Rachel Trezise was born in the Rhondda Valley in South Wales, where she still lives. She studied at Glamorgan and Limerick Universities. Her novel *In and Out of the Goldfish Bowl* won a place on the Orange Futures List in 2002. *Harpers & Queen* magazine voted her New Face of Literature, 2003. In 2006 her first short fiction collection *Fresh Apples* won the Dylan Thomas Prize. She was writer in residence at the University of Texas, Austin in 2007. Her second short fiction collection *Cosmic Latte* was published by Parthian in 2013. Her work has been translated into several languages, including Macedonian and Amharic. *Tonypandemonium,* her first full length play, was staged by National Theatre Wales in autumn 2013.

T0150606

TONYPANDEMONIUM

Rachel Trezise

Parthian
The Old Surgery
Napier Street
Cardigan
SA43 1ED
www.parthianbooks.com

First published in 2014
Tonypandemonium © Rachel Trezise
All Rights Reserved

ISBN 978-1-909844-76-6

The publisher acknowledges the financial support of the Welsh Books Council.

Cover design and typesetting by Claire Houguez
Cover image © National Theatre Wales
Photo section images © Mark Douet / National Theatre Wales

Printed and bound by lightningsource.com

British Library Cataloguing in Publication Data

A cataloguing record for this book is available from the British Library.

CONTENTS

Foreword by John McGrath   vii

Tonypandemonium   1

Photosection   81

FOREWORD

Two of the first books I picked up to read when I was
appointed Artistic Director of the new National Theatre Wales
were collections of short stories by Rhondda writers – Gwyn
Thomas and Rachel Trezise. I immediately wanted to put
both writers on stage. Thomas (1913-1981) had written plays
– but it was the anarchic comedy of his stories that I longed to
see theatricalised – a feat achieved for NTW by Paul Hunter
and Carl Grose in 2010 using the most physical storytelling
imaginable. Rachel had adapted her own work into scripts,
and her book *Fresh Apples* was being theatricalised in English
and Welsh – but my wish with Rachel was to see her write an
original play. I felt strongly that theatre, in and beyond Wales,
needed her voice – as harsh and yet hilarious in its unique
way as Thomas's. And I hoped that if I could get her to write
one play, she would go on to write many more.

It took a while. Rachel Trezise is a busy writer and she
doesn't do things lightly. It was about six months after I
first offered to commission her that she said yes; and then
she started her research, among other things coming to see
NTW's work in its opening season – and responding with
excitement and a sense of intrigue to productions such as
Gary Owen's *Love Steals Us From Loneliness* and that Thomas
adaptation, *The Dark Philosophers*. She started sending me

ideas – usually brief scenes from possible plays. Initial versions included none of the characters seen in the final script, and yet there was one consistent element; the title, *Tonypandemonium*. It was as though that word summed up everything she was searching for in her play – a combination of wit, raucous energy and local savvy.

Eventually, Rachel decided that home was were the heart should be for her first piece of theatre, and she retuned to one of her most consistent themes – a girl dealing with her wild, unpredictable mother – a heartbroken love letter to a wayward parent. There are direct links to the world of many of her stories, and to her celebrated first novel, *In and Out of the Goldfish Bowl*. Yet this is not an adaptation of that material, it's something with a very different life of its own – summed up in that most public of titles *Tonypandemonium*. In her play, Rachel places alcoholic mother Deborah and long-suffering, rebellious, infatuated, contradictory daughter Danielle, in a world in which they can make a kind of sense; a world of bewildered men obsessed by unlikely David Bowie sightings and car-stopping mini-skirts; a world where pennies that smell like blood are scraped together and then squandered; a world of survivors with wild imaginations. This is not a story of abuse behind closed doors, it's a story of a world off balance, sometimes gloriously so.

As the piece developed, I realised that Rachel was writing a play that took theatre itself very seriously. On the surface, the script could look like a domestic drama – reminiscent of the kitchen sink genre that Thomas had turned to in his play *The Keep* – or of much of today's television. But that title continued to give the clue: Rachel was creating a riot on stage – something that was shoving at the rules of well-made drama, breaking it out of shape. The daughter Danielle turned into three Danielles; the timeline shattered and folded in on itself; characters spoke to each other across the years and chatted to us like old friends. There were few rules of dramaturgy left to apply, but nonetheless we went through many drafts until a satisfyingly complete shape emerged.

Once we finally had a play, it was time to find the way to stage it. NTW was talking to the Park & Dare Theatre in Treorchy about how we could be part of the historic miners' institute's centenary celebrations. True to the 'wandering' ethos of NTW (which rehearses and stages productions all across Wales), we agreed that the theatre company should move into the building for a few months and put on a range of projects. While I'd originally planned to open *Tonypandemonium* in Cardiff, the prospect of opening the play at the Park & Dare Theatre quickly gained momentum – particularly once Rachel explained that she could actually walk from her house to the Park & Dare in less than five minutes. And so *Tonypandemonium* came home.

Aware of what a theatrical world Rachel had created within her local and domestic story, I asked Mathilde López if she would direct. Mathilde has a rare talent for combining unexpected stage experimentation with an instinct for how to engage an audience. Theatre for her is a direct, if very surprising, conversation between all the people in the room. She doesn't like or expect a quiet, well-behaved audience. Hailing from France via North Africa, Spain and the Caribbean, but resident in South Wales since she'd arrived as NTW Creative Associate four years prior, I felt she would give us the kind of theatrical pandemonium we needed.

Mathilde pushed the whole event to its logical conclusion. The theatre itself (in Jean Chan's inspired design) looked like a riot had hit it. The red velvet seats of the Park & Dare were boarded over and the entire space housed a mingling of audience and actors – with the fridges and sofas of the set scattered among us. The three Danielles in the script attracted a gang of followers – recruited from Treorchy Comprehensive School. Speeches in the play turned into stand-up routines, karaoke numbers, and intimate confessions whispered into microphones. *Tonypandemonium.*

And the audience loved it. Playing to packed houses every night – a mix of Treorchy folk who spotted every reference and others who were in the town for the first time in their lives – the production was bold, messy, raucous, moving, and a lot of fun to spend the night with. A bit like our lead character Deborah herself.

Deborah was embodied by Siwan Morris in an award-winning showstopper of a performance in which she lurched from a hospital bed to a tango with a rubber tree, to seduction of school teachers and school boys alike, to hilariously foul-mouthed abuse of all and sundry, to some of the best malapropisms I've ever heard!

It was a hell of a show – the kind of first production of a play that simultaneously makes you unable to imagine how it could be staged any other way – and yet equally fascinated to think that it might be. Or rather that it should be!

Because – although this is a play that demanded to be premiered amidst the South Wales Valleys community it celebrates and lacerates with a brilliance rarely seen since Gwyn Thomas achieved the same thing in a very different way – it also deserves to be seen in many different places, and staged in many different ways.

So I'm delighted that Parthian – in whose editions I read those short story collections by both Gwyn Thomas and Rachel Trezise when I was starting at NTW – are publishing the script of *Tonypandemonium.* I hope that it will reach many readers who will stage their own internal versions, but even more that it will entice producers, directors and performers to make versions for all of us.

And I'm equally delighted that Rachel seems to have caught the theatre bug – with new ideas already in development. I hope that she will continue to rip up the rules as beautifully, hilariously and movingly as she has in her first play.

John McGrath,
Artistic Director, National Theatre Wales

TONYPANDEMONIUM

Tonypandemonium was first performed on 10th October 2013, at the Park and Dare theatre in Treorchy, with the following cast:

DANIELLE #1 (9 years old)
/NURSE..Tamara Brabon
DANIELLE #2 (15 years old).....Molly Elson
DEBORAH.....................................Siwan Morris
TOMMY SIMCOX........................Adam Redmore
CRAIG/MR MORGAN..............Berwyn Pearce
JERRY DAVIES/LEON...............Dean Rehman
DANIELLE #3 (18 years old)....Sarah Williams

Directed by......................................Mathilde Lopez
Set Designer...................................Jean Chan
Lighting Designer........................Ceri James
Music and Sound Designer........Gareth Evans

1. TATTOO PARLOUR, PONTYPRIDD, 1996

TOMMY: *(Embarrassed)* Oh, sorry lovely. (Steps back behind the curtain.)

DANIELLE #3: It's OK, I'm just finishing up. *(Starts bandaging the customer up. Sends him out to reception.)*

(To Tommy) Come in.

TOMMY: Alright, love? Nice place you've got here. *(Looks around at the walls, intimidated.)* D'you think a tattoo would suit me, then? *(Shows Danielle his knuckles)* I could get love here on this hand, look, and hate here. All the things I did in my life, I never got a tattoo. Some of the boys did, on tour, y'know. I don't think I fancied the pain. *(Nervous laughter.)*

DANIELLE #3: *(Stern)* What? Just passing were you?

TOMMY: *(Coughs)* Your mother, it is.

DANIELLE #3: (Starts cleaning her gun) What's she done now?

TOMMY: Thing is, lovely — What it is — The hospital says she's only got about two weeks left.

DANIELLE #3: Two weeks? *(Confused)*

TOMMY: To live, love. Your mother's dying. She's dying, Dan.

DANIELLE #3: Dying? Fuck off. She's mean enough to live forever. What's she after?

TOMMY: I'm serious, love. Cirrhosis.

DANIELLE #3: Cirrhosis? I might have known.

TOMMY: Nothing they can do for her. *(Shrugs sadly.)* Ward 5, East Glam. It's not far from here. *(Beat.)* Will you go to see her, lovely?

DANIELLE #3: Has she asked? *(TOMMY shakes his head.)* Then why should I?

TOMMY: She won't ask. You know what she's like — It doesn't mean she doesn't want to see you. She's dying, love. She knows she's dying. She doesn't know how long; she doesn't want to know. Two weeks. If she knew she'd ask.

DANIELLE #3: *(Angry)* She's only forty-four.

TOMMY: I know.

DANIELLE #2: *(Shouting from off stage)* Next customer is in, Dan. Butterfly anklet?

TOMMY: Time for me to go anyway, lovely. Shopping, I am. New nightie and Turkish Delights. Got a real thing for the chocolate these days, she has. Have a think. *(Pats Danielle's shoulder awkwardly.)* See you then, lovely. *(Exits)*

RECEPTIONIST: *(Shouting from off stage)* Yoo-hoo. Ready?

2. KITCHEN IN A TERRACED HOUSE, TONYPANDY, 1987

DANIELLE #1: What's this?

DEBORAH: *(Nods at the empty chair)* Go on, I've made your breakfast. You need some substanance, don't you? Growing girl like you.

DANIELLE #1: Substanance isn't a word.

DEBORAH: Yes it is. Substanance. Like nutritions.

DANIELLE #1: Nutritions isn't either.

DEBORAH: Sit down.

DANIELLE #3: *(Chewing her Mars Bar. To Danielle #1)* She wasn't much of a cook. It all came out of tins and packets. Don't think I'd tasted a real potato. She used the freeze dried stuff. I can't remember what we did before Tommy got the microwave for us, cheap from Bessemer Road. It was alright for her. Lived on Turkish Delight, she did. Like the ice queen of Narnia. My father tried to teach her but — *(Too tired to explain. Slumps into the empty chair between DANIELLE #1 and DEBORAH.)*

DEBORAH: Think you can do me a favour now I've fed you up nice and full?

DANIELLE #1: *(Sighs)* I knew it! What now?

DEBORAH: Run down the big pine end house on the
              main road.

DANIELLE #1: Why? I've got combined science at nine
              o'clock with Mr Morgan. I'm making a
              grandfather clock out of a Weetabix box.
              With a pendulum in it and everything.

DEBORAH: Go on. It won't take you five minutes. I
              threw my shoes in the garden on my way
              home last night. My best ones. My leopard
              print ones.

DANIELLE #1: Why did you do that?

DEBORAH: My feet were tired.

DANIELLE #1: You could have carried them.

*TOMMY SIMCOX enters. DEBORAH puts her leopard-print
shoes on and joins him.*

TOMMY: Well this happened back when I was
              working on the railways in London, see. I
              was on my way to meet my mucker in this
              pub we'd been going to. Myfanwy's, it was
              called; Welsh place off Holloway Road.
              They'd let you smoke a bit of wacky backy
              in the cubby, like. I was walking past this
              theatre and all the audience were spilling
              out onto the street, hundreds of people. All
              of a sudden, there's David Bowie. Right in
              front of me, in the flesh. The eyes, everything.
              So, I shook his hand, like. 'Alright, Dave?
              Nice to meet you, butt.' And he just sort
              of disappeared back into the crowd. Later
              on, me and this mate, we're coming out of

Myfanwy's. Two o'clock in the morning.
There's David Bowie again, stood in the
middle of the road. He's just standing there
on his own, whistling this tune, looking a bit
lost, like. I swear to God. And that's when he
started stalking me. The whole time I lived in
London. I couldn't go to the shop to get milk
without him turning up like a bad penny.
Caught him once, up on the extension roof,
staring through the bathroom window.

DEBORAH: *(Taking her shoes off)* Stupid bloody things.
Killing me. (Throws them). .

TOMMY: Watching me have a shower. Fucking
Bowie, like.

(Catches her) Oh, bloody hell, love. I'm too
old for this.

DEBORAH: What? I'm only light. *(Covers TOMMY's
eyes.)*

TOMMY: *(Walking unsteadily.)* Whoa! Whoa, you
nutter. Can't see where I'm going.
(DEBORAH laughing, removes her hands.)
Good job I fancy you, aye. Banger short of a
barbeque you are, love.

DEBORAH: **Fancy** me, do you?

TOMMY: And the rest.

DANIELLE #1: *(Clicks her tongue)* You could have hurt
yourself.

DEBORAH: *(Impatient)* It's only half past eight. Go on,
sweetheart. They'll still be there.

DANIELLE #1: You go. They're **your** shoes. You threw them
away. Why'd you throw them away?

9

DEBORAH: *(Shouts)* Because— *(Takes the breakfast to the bin, starts scraping the plate)*

DANIELLE #1: OK! But this is the last time. *(Under her breath)* Things you have to do around here for a quiet life. *(Exits)*

DEBORAH: *(Daydreaming and talking to herself)* 'And the rest.' Seven years younger than me, he is. See, I've still got it. Everywhere I go, men tripping over their toes to get a sniff of me.

DANIELLE #1 returns with a baby's sock, puts it down on the table.

DANIELLE #1: They weren't there. All I could find was this, in the gutter.

DEBORAH: Well, did you have a proper look?

DANIELLE #1: *(Playing with the sock)* Yeah! And then I had to run away because the man came out shouting at me for being on 'private property' or something.

DEBORAH: They're my best shoes. The leopard-print ones from Oliver's. I paid for them myself!

DANIELLE #1: Someone must have taken them.

CRAIG: *(From offstage to DANIELLE #3)* Dan, what're you doing?

DANIELLE #1: Perhaps your boyfriend went back to get them. Present for his wife. Finder's keepers.

DEBORAH: I'm only a size four! **That** woman's a size nine. Big boat feet like a man!

3. FAST FOOD RESTAURANT, PONTYPRIDD, 1992

JERRY: So how's your mother then, love?

DANIELLE #2: *(Shrugs)* Y'know —

JERRY: What did you tell her?

DANIELLE #2: I told her I was ice-skating with Katie in Cardiff. Believe anything won't she?

JERRY: It's for the best, love. If she knew you were with me she'd have my knackers off. You know what she's like —

DANIELLE #2: Yeah, I know what she's like. I'm the one who has to live with her.

JERRY: She seeing anyone now then, love?

DANIELLE #2: Tommy Simcox. *(JERRY looks hurt.)*

Off and on, like. She sends him home to his wife every other weekend, then, when she wants him back she gets all dressed up and goes looking for him round the pubs. Wears her best fur coat.

JERRY: Never satisfied, is she?

DANIELLE #2: I want to come and live with you, Dad.

JERRY: You know that's difficult, love. I'm with Margaret now. She's a stickler for a clean and tidy house. She drives me mad half the time.

DANIELLE #2: Not a nutcase though, is she?

JERRY: Don't say that about your mother, love. She's got a heart of gold.

DEBORAH: *(From offstage)* Stop drawing on the furniture!

JERRY: Fragile, she is— It's hard to explain.

DANIELLE #2: She's mental, Dad. And you know it. She totalled your car. She had the injunction taken out. She ruins everything. Everything she touches she turns to shit. Everything she's had, she's pissed all over it.

JERRY: You shouldn't be so hard on her, love. She can't help it. Always been the same; selfish, self-centred. She cuts her nose off to spite her own face. She doesn't do it on purpose, love. She doesn't know any other way.

DANIELLE #2: It's not fair, Dad. She's pissed all the time. Thursday night she had Shirley Bassey on blaring 'til four in the morning. I had a maths test the next day. That's not right, is it? It's like she's the kid and I have to be the mother.

JERRY: I'll have to talk to Margaret, love. You have to see things from her point of view. She hasn't got any children. It's a lot to ask, a strange teenager in the house.

DANIELLE #2: I'm not a stranger, Dad. I'm your daughter.

JERRY: You know what I mean, love —

DANIELLE #2: She said you'd do this. She said you
            wouldn't want me. It's only her you care
            about. Every time I see you she's all you go
            on about. 'How's your mother? Who's she
            seeing?' Obsessed with her, you are. You
            don't even care about me.

JERRY: I'll talk to Margaret.

DANIELLE #2: It's not going to be for long. I'm nearly
            sixteen. I've got to do my exams, then I can
            get my own flat.

JERRY: It's the cleaning thing it is, love. She's awful
            strict.

DANIELLE #2: She won't even know I'm there. I can help
            her with the cleaning. Who do you think
            does the cleaning up there? It's not my
            mother, is it? It's not Tommy bloody
            Simcox.

JERRY: We'll see.

DANIELLE #2: That means yes.

JERRY: It means we'll see. Because you know
            there'll be trouble. You know she'll kick off.

4. BEDROOM, TERRACED HOUSE, TONYPANDY, 1987

DANIELLE #1 is playing with dolls; a dark-haired Barbie, a light-haired Barbie, an Action Man and a Flower Fairy. She's acting out a scenario, holding them up to face one another and speaking for them in different voices and tones.

DANIELLE #1 *(DARK-HAIRED DOLL/DANIELLE #2 join in on underlined)*: Uncle Tommy doesn't love you because you're <u>a slut</u> and a single mother. You stole your ex-husband's car and got away with it because you slept with the copper who arrested you. You're not right in the head, love. All fur coat and no knickers.

DANIELLE#1 *(LIGHT-HAIRED DOLL/DANIELLE #2 join in on underlined)*: Shut your mouth, <u>you fat bitch</u>. And guess what? He does love me. Because why would he love you? You've got three chins and enough fat on your arse to open a lipstick factory.

DANIELLE #1 *(DARK-HAIRED DOLL/DANIELLE #3 join in on the underlined)*: <u>And you're ill, love</u>. An alcoholic. You should be in Bridgend with your sister.

DANIELLE #1 *(LIGHT-HAIRED DOLL/DANIELLE #2 join in on the underlined:* Oh, mind your own business. <u>Jealous cow. I don't ask you to pay for my drinks, do I?</u>

14

DANIELLE #1 *(DARK-HAIRED DOLL/DANIELLE #3 join in on underlined):*   No, you ask my husband, darling. Anyway, <u>let's ask Tommy who he loves</u>. Who do you love, Uncle Tommy? Which one of us do you love?

DANIELLE #1/ACTION MAN FIGURE:
One woman man, I am. You know me mun, love. You're a bit confused aren't you, Debs? Had a bit too much to drink?

DANIELLE # 2/DANIELLE #3:
You're a bloody liar, Tommy Simcox. A liar. You've always been full of shit, you. *(Cries)*

DANIELLE #1/FLOWER FAIRY DOLL:
Don't worry, Mammy. I love you. I love you more than Uncle Tommy. I love you more than anyone. No-one loves you more than me. I'll look after you, I will. I'll save you, Mammy.

DEBORAH enters.

DEBORAH: Don't you want to go out to play, sweetheart? Why don't you take your dolls up the park?

DANIELLE #1: I can't take my dolls up the park. The big girls'll steal them. It's raining anyway.

DEBORAH: I need the house to myself for a few hours, see. *(Beat.)* I know! There's a fancy dress competition in the church hall this afternoon. I saw a poster for it in the pub. Why don't you go to that?

DANIELLE #1: I haven't got a fancy dress costume. I don't want to anyway. I'm playing house.

DEBORAH: What do you want to go as? We can make a
                fancy dress costume for you.

DANIELLE #1: I don't want to go to a fancy dress
                competition.

DEBORAH: Indian? Cowboy? I know! A Charleston girl!
                I've got a dress somewhere with fringes
                like the Charleston girls used to wear. And
                we'll put an ostrich feather in your hair?
                Yeah!

DANIELLE #1: What's a Charleston girl?

DEBORAH: *(Impatient)* Oh, it's these girls from the 1920s
                and they used to dance like this *(does the
                dance)*. Come on, we'll get you all dressed
                up and when you go in you have to dance
                like this *(does the dance)*. Bet you any money
                you'll win.

DANIELLE #1: I'm not dancing like that.

DEBORAH: But you'll win.

DANIELLE #1: I don't want to win. I'm playing house.

DEBORAH: Come on, sweetheart. Be a good girl now.
                Mammy's got things to do, see. Private
                things, grown up things. There you are,
                look. *(Turns Danielle to face the mirror.)*

DANIELLE #1: I look stupid. I've never seen one of these
                Charleston girls before. Nobody'll know
                what I'm meant to be.

DEBORAH: You look brilliant! You do. Do the dance
                then.

DANIELLE #1: Nuh!

DEBORAH: Go on, do the dance. More chance of winning!

DANIELLE #1: No! *(Pulls the feather out of her hair)*

DEBORAH: *(Puts the feather back in)* Come on, sweetheart. Please? I need the house for an hour, that's all. You can take your dolls with you, mun. Go on, you might win.

DANIELLE #1: I'm not going to win. They won't even know what I am. How's the vicar going to know what a Charleston girl is?

DEBORAH: He will. Go on. You won't know if you don't try. You can have one of my Turkish Delights when you come back.

DANIELLE#1: This is stupid, this is.

DEBORAH: But you might win.

DANIELLE #1: I won't win.

DEBORAH: Go on. *(Waving her off)* Remember to do the dance.

5. LIVING ROOM, TERRACED HOUSE, TONYPANDY, 1992

TOMMY arrives home from work carrying his hard hat and lunchbox to find DEBORAH sitting on the settee drinking a glass of vodka. She's quite slurry.

TOMMY: Started early haven't you, love?

DEBORAH: Not like I've got much else to do, is it? Not like I've got any kids to look after.

TOMMY: *(Exhausted)* So, are you hungry? I'll pop down Conti's for chips again, is it?

DEBORAH: Whatever.

6. ALLEYWAY, TONYPANDY, 1992

DANIELLE #2: Let's have a can 'en.

LEON: Blow job first.

DANIELLE #2: As if.

LEON: Your mother would.

DANIELLE #2: I'm not my mother, am I?

LEON: *(To CRAIG)* Danielle's mother was the kissogram in my cousin's 30th.

DANIELLE #3: *(To DANIELLE #2)* Better than poisoning rats for a living.

LEON: Is that what you're going to be, Dan? A stripper? *(Giggling)*

DANIELLE #3: Which is what he's going to end up doing.

DANIELLE #2: *(Glaring at LEON)* 'Least she's not a Jehovah's Witness. What are you having for Christmas, Lee?

CRAIG: Fucking hell, Dan. He can't choose what religion his parents are.

DANIELLE #2: Yeah, and I can choose who my mother is, can I?

CRAIG: Who would you choose though?

DANIELLE #2: Easy. Sally Field out of *Steel Magnolias.*

DANIELLE #3: Aww. *(Grimaces)* Too sweet.

LEON: Madonna.

CRAIG: For your mother? Weirdo. Leon's got his father's Malibu, Dan.

DANIELLE #2: Come on then, Lee.

LEON: Nah, get your own. You owe me half a bottle as it is.

DANIELLE #2: She's moved her stash, mun. I think she's onto me.

CRAIG: Try the toilet. You know, the cistern. I saw it on TV. It's an alkie's favourite place to hide their booze. *(Danielle looks at him, hurt.)*

LEON: Neck me for it.

DANIELLE #3: *(Looking up in disgust.)* Don't neck him.

CRAIG: Don't neck him, Dan.

DANIELLE #2: Go on then.

DANIELLE #2 looks pointedly at CRAIG before moving in to kiss LEON, stopping short at the last moment; meanwhile CRAIG takes the bottle of Malibu out of LEON's pocket. DANIELLE #2 moves away again. CRAIG throws the bottle to her and she catches it. She stands up and starts drinking from it.

LEON:	*(Opening his eyes and getting up to chase Danielle)* Come on, Dan. It's mine.
CRAIG:	That's the third time you've fallen for that. How gullible are you, mun?
LEON:	*(Following DANIELLE around and around the stage)* You've had some now, Dan. Give it back. *(To CRAIG)* This is your fault, Craig. You'll do anything she tells you, because you fancy her. You're like her little puppy dog or something mun.
CRAIG:	*(Embarrassed)* No I don't.
LEON:	Yes you do. You told me you want to finger her. *(To Danielle)* You want to neck me really. Just frigid.
DANIELLE #2:	Yeah. Frigid when it comes to you, Lee. I'm scared of your little pencil dick, I am.
LEON:	Why are you such a bitch, mun?
DANIELLE #2:	You think I'm a bitch? You should meet my mother. Oh, you already have, haven't you? I almost forgot.
DANIELLE #3:	You're turning into her.
DANIELLE #2:	What?
DANIELLE #3:	You're turning into your mother. She's teaching you how to manipulate people. She's teaching you how to manipulate men. You want Malibu? Buy it. Get a paper round or something. You don't kiss boys to get what you want. What does that make you?
DANIELLE #2:	I didn't kiss him.

DANIELLE #3: So you're a tease as well? *(Beat.)* Go home. It's cold. You'll catch a cold. *(Pushes her off set. Takes a swig of the Malibu and makes a face)* Nah, I never did like rum. *(Throws the bottle back to LEON. Approaches CRAIG and holds his chin. Kisses him forcefully on the mouth. Exits)*

CRAIG: Dan!

LEON: She's got you wrapped around her little finger, butt. Fuckin' cock tease bitch.

CRAIG: *(Dazed)* She's alright, mun, Lee. Give her a break.

LEON: Hark at Prince fuckin' Charmin'. No chance, butt. She's a lesbian, I reckon, like her auntie. She's either a lesbian or a slag.

CRAIG: Which one?

LEON: I don't know, do I? Both.

7. LIVING ROOM, TERRACED HOUSE, TONYPANDY, 1987

DANIELLE #2: *(Not looking up from the magazine)* The thing with our mother; she was always trying to get us out of the house. *(DANIELLE #1 turns to look at her)*

DEBORAH: *(Puts the phone down)* Don't you want to go out to play, sweetheart? Come on. I need the house to myself for a few hours. Don't you want to go up to the park to play? Take the skateboard Uncle Tommy got for you in the market?

DANIELLE #1: It's raining.

DEBORAH: Well there must be something you can do. Go on, I've got things to sort out here.

DANIELLE #1: What things?

DANIELLE #2: You don't want to know.

DANIELLE #1: It's raining, Mam. Morph'll be on now. I've only just come in.

DEBORAH: What about that St. John's Ambulance Club in the Legion? You're interested in First Aid, aren't you?

DANIELLE #2: Jesus wept.

DANIELLE #1: No!

DEBORAH: Come on, Danni. Don't make trouble for
             me tonight. I need the house to myself.
             Only for a couple of hours. I've got things
             to do. Private things. Grown-up things.

DEBORAH: Go to the St. John's Ambulance Club. Just
             this once. For Mammy. You might like it.

DANIELLE #2: She won't like it! *(Beat.)* You've got to be
             thirteen!

DANIELLE #1: You've got to be thirteen to join St. John's
             Ambulance. It's only for kids from the
             comp. And it costs a pound. I don't want to
             go anyway. I won't like it.

DEBORAH: *(Tips a jar of copper coins onto the table and
             begins to count them)* Go on, sweetheart. I'll
             give you a pound.

DANIELLE #1: I'm not paying in two pence's. It's
             embarrassing.

DEBORAH: It's all I've got. It's just the same as a pound
             coin, but different. Seventy, eighty.

DANIELLE #1: I can't go to St John's Ambulance, Mam.

DEBORAH: *(To Audience member)* C'mon, can you lend
             me 10p love?

DANIELLE #1: You've got to be thirteen.

DEBORAH: Be a good girl for Mammy now.

DANIELLE #1: I'm only nine.

DANIELLE #2: She's only nine.

DEBORAH: Please, love. Go. Just this once. For me. Just this once. Mammy's got things to do, see. I've got a few things to sort out. Please, sweetheart. It's important. *(Hands the coins to DANIELLE #1)*

DANIELLE #1: *(Sniffing the coins)* Smell these do.

DEBORAH: It's all I've got.

DANIELLE #1: I can't go, Mam. They'll know I'm not thirteen. They'll know I'm lying. I'll stay in my bedroom. I won't come out.

DEBORAH: They won't know how old you are. You're tall for your age, aren't you? If they ask, all you've got to do is tell them your date of birth but with the year changed so it works out at thirteen.

DANIELLE #1: What is it?

DANIELLE #2: '75. 1975.

DANIELLE #1: *(To DEBORAH)* 1975.

DEBORAH: See, you're cleverer than half those kids from the comp, gul. Come on, sweetheart. Be a good girl.

DANIELLE #1: I can't believe you're making me do this.

DEBORAH: I can't believe you're being cheeky to your poor mother.

DANIELLE #1: *(Sniffing the coins)* Smell these do, like blood.

CRAIG: *(To DANIELLE #3)* How did it go Dan?

DEBORAH: It's all I've got. Be a good girl now.

DANIELLE #1: I am a good girl. It's you who's making me tell lies.

DEBORAH: Go on then sweetheart. You never know, you might like it.

DANIELLE #2: *(Shouts)* She won't like it!

DEBORAH: Go on, you might learn something. They'll teach you the discovery position, isn't it?

DANIELLE #2: *(Sighs)* Go on, it's only an hour.

8. KITCHEN, TERRACED HOUSE, TONYPANDY, 1992

DEBORAH: Oh, I was the best jiver around when I was younger. Debbie rock 'n' roll they used to call me up the Polikoff's Club.

TOMMY: *(Noticing DANIELLE)* Oh, where d'you come from, lovely?

DANIELLE #2: The front door.

DEBORAH: Don't be smart, girl.

TOMMY: *(Lifts the towel from the basket, looking inside)* What's this, then?

DANIELLE #2: Rice and veg and stuff. It's called Risotto Primavera or somin'. Cookery teacher's from the Vale, thinks she's posh.

TOMMY: Bloody hell, lovely. I know what it is. Practically lived off this stuff when I was working on the canals in Italy, I did. There was this little osteria around the corner from our hostel. All they served was risotto. Donkey risotto, mind. Look at that! Have this for tea tonight, is it?

DEBORAH: *(Eyeing DANIELLE jealously)* I'm making my corned beef pie tonight. May as well put that out for the birds.

TOMMY: Corned beef pie? When's the last time
              you made corned beef pie, Debs? Thought
              I was going down Conti's for chips again.
              You can do pie anytime. *(To DANIELLE)*
              Put it in the oven, lovely.

DEBORAH: *(Moving to block the oven door.)* What's in
              it, then?

DANIELLE #2: Beans, carrots, onions, cheese, tomatoes —

DEBORAH: Well there you are. I can't eat that. I'm
              allergic to tomatoes. It's their skin, it
              irritates my throat. You now that. Chuck it
              out for the birds, gul. It'll only get left in the
              fridge, going off, cluttering up. I'm doing
              my corned beef pie. I've been planning it
              for days. *(Beat.)* What? Don't look at me
              like that. I've bought all the ingredients.

TOMMY: That's going to take ages, love. Stick a bowl
              of Danni's risotto in the oven for me while
              I'm waiting. I'm starving.

DEBORAH: No, I'm not having you spoiling my corned
              beef pie with that foreign rubbish, Tom.

DANIELLE #2: Jesus. It's not foreign. I made it in school.
              Llewellyn Street. Half a mile away.

DEBORAH: You know what I mean, sweetheart. It's too
              rich. He hasn't got the stomach for it.

DANIELLE #2: He likes risotto. He just said.

DEBORAH: Listen, I don't know who he was sleeping
              next to when he lived away but I'm not
              putting up with his rich food farts all night,
              alright?

DANIELLE #2: You think the whole world revolves around you, you do. You're jealous because I cooked a risotto. Pathetic. I didn't even want to do it. The school made me do it. Ain't my fault Tommy wants to eat it. Any normal mother would want to eat their daughter's food from cookery.

DEBORAH: *(Peeling potatoes, sipping vodka)* Me? Jealous of you? I don't know what you're talking about, Danielle. What have you got that I'd be jealous of? Duller than you look you are, girl. And pick up your drawings!

DANIELLE #2: Yeah, right. I'm going to change. *(Exits)*

TOMMY: Corned beef pie? Vegetable Risotto? Do me a favour. I'd kill now for one of my ex-Mrs' beef Wellingtons. Debs, right? She wasn't my first choice. I got caught cheating, didn't I? Stuck with her. It's like walking on egg shells, mun. *(Looking back to the kitchen, slightly worried)* Last weekend she kicked me out for eating her chocolate. Turkish Delight. I don't even like the bastard stuff. *(Makes a face)* Sweet pink jelly, sickly as hell. Starvin', I was. And she flushed my signed Stones plectrum down the lav. Keith Richards gave that to me, personally. Personally, mind. Richmond Athletic Ground 1964.

Knew she was trouble, first time I saw her. Debs was the kissogram at my stag do. My mate hired her for fifty quid. Couldn't resist, could I? Stunning. Only human, I am. Moth to a flame, like. So here I am. Happy bloody families. Daren't go back to the ex. I mean there's only so many times I can afford to put the car in for a respray.

DANIELLE #2 enters wearing a Guns 'n' Roses T-shirt and a pair of clumpy motorbike boots.

TOMMY: *(Spying DANIELLE over the paper)* Nice boots, lovely.

DEBORAH: *(Shouting from the kitchen)* Don't encourage her, Tommy. Ugliest things I've had the displeasure of seeing on a human being's feet. Years ago I couldn't keep her away from my shoes. Now she wants to dress like a feller. Can't get a skirt on her for love nor money. People'll be thinking my daughter's a Lesbos.

DANIELLE #2: Lesbian! It's lesbian! Lesbos is an island. Off Greece. Fuck's sake.

TOMMY: You like Thin Lizzy then, lovely?

DANIELLE #2: Prefer Metallica, Tom.

TOMMY: Me 'n' Pete the papers were roadies for Thin Lizzy, see. Back in London, good few years ago. Those were the days, love. Touring with Slade. Me 'n' old Gary Moore were like that. *(Crosses fingers. Breaks into song and plays air guitar)* **Guess who just got back today** — Taught me a lot, that Phil Lynnott. Black kid growing up in 1940s Ireland. Can you imagine the stick he must have got? Never complained about it, not once. Gave me the strength to forgive all the shit I had to endure around here for having one arm longer than the other.

DEBORAH: *(Shouting)* Come on, it's ready. *(Beat.)* I didn't have any carrots. Or onions. Got everything else though. C'mon, tuck in.

DANIELLE #2: Got all the ingredients you said.

TOMMY: Like corned beef hash then love, but in a
           pie? Nice one. *(Pats DEB's shoulder proudly.)*

DEBORAH: I'm good, aren't I? Creative, see. Cooking's
           creative. I'm awful creative. I can turn my
           hand to anything creative. They thought I
           was going to be a hairdresser. My father used
           to let me cut his hair from the time I was six.
           I'd just sit on his lap with a scissors doing
           whatever I wanted to him, soft old sod.

DANIELLE #2: Baking's a science.

DEBORAH: Remember, Dan? When I made a fancy
           dress costume for that competition in the
           church hall? Dressed her up as a flapper
           with my old fringed dress. Two minutes
           it took me. Couple of feathers. She only
           bloody won. First bloody prize.

TOMMY: Never. What d'you win, lovely?

DANIELLE #2: Five pack of Mars Bars. Wish I had five
           Mars Bars here now. I'd eat them all, instead
           of this. Your potatoes are like rocks. How
           can you have a corned beef pie without
           onions, anyway? Baking is a science. You
           follow a recipe. There's no creativity in it.
           You couldn't bake a jam tart, Mam.

DEBORAH: Watch your mouth, girl. I didn't use a
           recipe. I did it from memory. You're not too
           big for a clout.

DANIELLE #2: Mam, you're lucky you can see me, you're
           that drunk. Hit the one in the middle, is it?

DEBORAH: I can see you alright, girl. *(Stands up)*

TOMMY: Not tonight, ladies. C'mon. Calm down.
                Let's eat our tea in peace for once, is it?

DANIELLE #2:   I'm not eating this. *(Picks her plate up)*
                Where's my risotto?

DEBORAH: You can't eat that now. I've put it out for
                the birds.

DANIELLE #2:   Well, what d'you do that for?

TOMMY: You shouldn't have put it out for the birds,
                love. Rice, see. It expands in their stomachs.
                (Beat.) It makes them spontaneously combust.

DANIELLE #2:   She shouldn't have put it out for the birds
                because it's my fucking risotto. *(To
                DEBORAH)* You're not right in the head,
                you ain't. A normal person would not put a
                perfectly good risotto out for the birds. Let
                alone their own daughter's!

TOMMY: Don't swear in front of your mother, lovely.

DANIELLE #2:   She fuckin' swears in front of me.

DEBORAH: *(Shoving to get closer to DANIELLE)* I've had
                as much of your lip as I can take today,
                madam. I'll teach you a lesson now.

DANIELLE #2:   I've had as much as I can take from you in a
                lifetime. Mental hospital you ought to be,
                with your sister.

DEBORAH: Don't talk about my sister.

DANIELLE #2:   *(Exasperated)* Out for the birds? What have I
                ever done to you?

DEBORAH: Implored me, you have. For fifteen long
                years you've been imploring me. I tell you,

I should have listened to that doctor!

DANIELLE #2: Imploring you? You don't even know what that means. Provoking you. Provoke, you stupid cow. I can't even have an argument with you. You're too thick.

TOMMY: Love? Don't swear at your mother.

DANIELLE #2: Don't you tell me what to do either. You must be mental to stay with her. Going to live with my father, I am.

DEBORAH: Try it, Danielle. He doesn't want you. When was the last time you saw him? Twelve years ago. He doesn't want you.

DANIELLE #2: Why's that, Mam? Because you had an injunction taken out on him.

DEBORAH: Yes, because he beat me up.

DANIELLE #2: He didn't beat you up. Tommy's ex-wife beat you up. Then you used the photographs to say it was my father, because you're psychotic like that, aren't you? *(To TOMMY)* That's a true story, that is. Bet she never told you that one.

DEBORAH: That's **it**, girl.

DANIELLE #2: I'm going anyway.

TOMMY: Don't go, lovely. Where are you going to go? Sit down, mun. We can sort this out.

DANIELLE #2: We can't sort this out until she's stopped drinking. She won't even remember this tomorrow. I'm sick of her starting on me for nothing. Then she won't apologize because

she can't even remember what she's done.
She's going to give me a nervous breakdown.
I'm trying to revise for my exams.

DEBORAH: Let her go. I'm sick of the sight of her and
her stupid, ugly boots. Get out, you spoiled
little bitch.

DANIELLE #2: Me a spoiled bitch? You should fucking see
yourself. What kind of woman gives her
own daughter's risotto to the birds? Wake
up. You're not what you think you are.
You're not a little girl competing with your
sisters for your father's attention. You're a
grown woman. You've got a fifteen-year-
old daughter. Who's brainier than you.

DEBORAH: *(Upset)* Don't talk about my sisters.

TOMMY: OK, lovely. Perhaps you'd better go out for
an hour, cool down, like.

DANIELLE #2: I'm going. *(Exits carrying her plate.)* Watch
the birds spontaneously combust after this
shit. *(Smashes the dish off stage.)*

9. EAST GLAMORGAN
HOSPITAL, WARD 5, 1996

DANIELLE #3: Mother?

DEBORAH: *(Disappointed)* You.

DANIELLE #3: Yeah me, Mam.

DEBORAH: How did you find out? Bloody Tommy,
              wasn't it? Couldn't keep his mouth shut. I
              don't want you coming here. I don't want
              your bloody sympathy.

DANIELLE #3: Who said anything about sympathy?
              Cirrhosis of the liver? It's your own fault.

DEBORAH: *(Turns her head away)* Anyway, it's not even
              visiting time. You'd better go before the
              nurses catch you. They're strict. *(Turns back,
              looking hesitantly at DANIELLE.)* I don't want
              them seeing you, truth be told. You look like
              a tramp off the street, gul. Ripped jeans?
              Come to see your mother in hospital and
              you can't even be bothered to wear a dress.

DANIELLE #3: *(Sarcastic)* And you look beautiful.
              Gorgeous as ever. Prettier than Elizabeth
              Taylor, you are.

DEBORAH: Shut it you. You've still got a mouth on you.
               I thought you might have grown up a bit
               by now. I can't help what I look like. I'm ill!

DANIELLE #3:   *(Quietly)* Yeah. *(Looks down at her jeans.)* I
               came straight from work.

DEBORAH: Well you shouldn't have bothered. You
               know better than to listen to Tommy. You
               know he's full of shit. He's the one looking
               for sympathy, feeling sorry for himself
               because there's no-one there to cook for
               him when he gets in. It's not as bad as he's
               making out. I'll be OK. I always am. Have
               to be, don't I? The liver is the only organ
               capable of repairing itself. So actually it's
               a good job it's not cancer like the rest of
               them. Your grancha died of lung cancer.
               Terrible thing. They reckoned it was his
               smoking but it wasn't. It was the coalmines
               that killed him. Bloody NBC. I sat next to
               his bed watching him getting worse day
               after day, sinking into himself 'til there was
               nothing left of the poor dab.

DANIELLE #3:   Well I thought you might have wanted
               some company. You hate hospitals, you
               always did. You wouldn't even go in to have
               me. Thought you might have been lonely.

DEBORAH: I'm not lonely, thank you very much. I've
               made hundreds of friends here. And I've got
               the nurses. At least they look after me. Not
               like you with your ripped jeans and your
               dirty boots. You told me you weren't going
               to look after me when I got old so I don't
               know why you've bothered coming now.

DANIELLE #3:   You're not old. Anyway, you didn't look
               after me.

DEBORAH: I did my best.

DANIELLE #3: No you didn't.

DEBORAH: *(Stern)* I'm too ill to argue with you,
                Danielle. I'm tired. *(Shouts)* Nurse! Nurse!
                Intruder! Nurse!

DANIELLE #3: Don't be silly, Mam. Jesus Christ.
                Nurse *(DANIELLE #1)* enters carrying a kit,
                walks towards the bed.

NURSE: It's not visiting time. It ended over an hour
                ago. Can you come back tomorrow?

DANIELLE #3: *(Stands up)* I'll come back tomorrow.

NURSE: Time for your bandages now, Mrs. Simcox.
                (Begins bandaging)

DANIELLE #3: Do you want me to come back tomorrow,
                Mam?

NURSE: I'm sorry young lady, you really have to go
                now. It's almost nine o'clock.

DANIELLE #3: Do you want me to bring anything?

NURSE: The hospital should be empty of visitors by
                now.

DEBORAH: *(Shouting after her)* Danni? Turkish Delight.
                Turkish Delight. And cranberry juice.

10. TERRACED STREET, TONYPANDY, 1992.

DANIELLE #3: *(Looking around, making sure no-one's listening. To DANIELLE #2)* Hold your head up. Hold your head up. You've nothing to be ashamed of.

DANIELLE #2: *(Looking about, cross)* Nothing to be ashamed of? Are you real, or what?

DANIELLE #3: Yeah. *(Smiling)* Well, no.

DANIELLE #2: Stop fucking with my head. Why can't she just be normal? Why does it have to be me who gets the wino for a mother?

DANIELLE #3: Why not you? You're someone aren't you? Normal? No fucker's normal, babe. *(Beat.)* You'll be alright, you know. You're not the first teenage daughter of a dipso to walk the bloody earth. Look at me! Come on, get yourself home. She worries.

DANIELLE #2: *(Incredulous)* She does not worry.

DANIELLE #3: She does though. And go easy on her or it'll end up being one of those nights. She's on the change; temperamental as fuck. And you're on your period. Hormonal teenager and alcoholic mother under one terraced roof? Daddy's got a word for it.

LEON: Tonypandemonium.

DANIELLE #2: Fuck off! Bet she's through a bottle of vodka
                already, singing Shirley Bassey in the
                kitchen. *(Doing an impression of a drunken
                DEBORAH, singing)* **I, I who have nothing.
                I, I who have no-one.**

DANIELLE #3: *(Doing an impression of a drunken DEBORAH,
                singing)* **Diamonds are forever. They're all
                I need to please me. They can stimulate
                and tease me.**

DANIELLE #2: Don't you want to go out and play,
                sweetheart? Come on, I need the house
                to myself for a few hours. Things to do.
                Private things. Grown up things.

DANIELLE #3: Why couldn't you have a normal job? Work
                in a pub or something. Tattoos! On women
                as well! You've got to have a screw loose to
                want to mark your body like that, mun.

DANIELLE #2: I should have listened to that doctor! Party
                girl, I am!

DANIELLE #3: See, I've still got it. Everywhere I go, men
                tripping over themselves to get a good look
                at me. Prettier than Elizabeth Taylor, I was.
                She ain't got nothing on me. Fat Jewish tart.

DANIELLE #2: Oh, Danni, look at your big ugly shoes.
                People'll think you're a lesbos. A Lesbos,
                mun. You might find a nice boyfriend if
                you wear prettier shoes.

DANIELLE #3: *(Laughing)* Come on.

11. LIVING ROOM, TERRACED HOUSE, TONYPANDY, 1987

DEBORAH: *(Into the telephone receiver, sighing)* Yes, this is the Jade Flower. How can I help you, sweetheart? *(Pause; winks at DANIELLE #1.)* Black bean sauce, yep— Egg fried Rice, yep— Four poppadums, yep— And a bag of chips? Big or small? Ok no problem, I'll just pass you onto my colleague who can check your order.

DANIELLE #1: Ok so that's black bean sauce, egg fried rice, four poppadums' and a small bag of chips? Are you sure you want a small bag? If you buy a big bag you can have a free Barbie with every chip...

DEBORAH: That'll teach them for dialling the wrong number again, silly buggers.

12. LIVING ROOM, TERRACED HOUSE, TONYPANDY, 1992

DEBORAH is in her nightdress, staring into space, when DANIELLE #2 enters. They're both drunk and their speech is slurred.

DEBORAH: You OK, sweetheart? Where've you been then?

DANIELLE #2: Out. You threw me out, remember?

DEBORAH: Did I? I didn't, did I?

DANIELLE #2: Huh. Yeah.

DEBORAH: No, I didn't, mun. I wouldn't do that. You're my favourite girl, you are. Do you know when I was having you the doctor thought you were a virus? 'Funny bloody virus, doc,' I told him. A virus with arms and legs! *(Beat.)* See, I knew I was pregnant. I knew. One Sunday I walked into my mother's house and she was cooking the dinner, and I loved her Sunday dinner. But ych-y-fi, the smell of it. Like something dead and rotting. 'I'm pregnant, I am,' I said to your father. 'Don't be silly,' he said. But I knew. And the doctor?

DEBORAH/ DANIELLE: He told me to have an abortion.

DEBORAH: 'If there's a baby there,' I said, 'It's staying there. It's staying put!'

DANIELLE #2: You wished you listened to that doctor. That's what you always tell me.

TOMMY: *(Shouting from off stage)* Debs? You coming to bed? It's late. Come to bed. Debs?

DEBORAH: *(Shouting to Tommy)* Alright, I'm coming, Tom. I'll be there now. Keep your cock on. *(To Danielle, quieter)* I don't mean that, sweetheart. You know the trouble I'm having with my hormones. I wouldn't abort a baby, I wouldn't. Not like that ex-of Tommy's. She's had abortions, she has. Calloused cow.

DANIELLE #2: Well maybe you should have. All you've done all my life is reject me, ignore me, humiliate me. Don't love me, do you?

DEBORAH: Do you remember that time —

DANIELLE #2: See, you can't say it. You can't even say it when you're pissed.

DEBORAH: Do you remember that time when you were little and I had to go to court?

DANIELLE #2: When you lied about my father beating you up?

DEBORAH: I didn't lie. You stayed with your grandparents.

DANIELLE #2: Yeah?

DEBORAH: Your grancha didn't—

DANIELLE #2: What?

DEBORAH: Your grancha didn't touch—

DANIELLE #2, [without catching what DEBORAH has said], begins to retch. DEBORAH slides a waste paper bin over to her and smoothes DANIELLE's hair to the side while DANIELLE vomits.

DEBORAH: There, there, sweetheart. Get it up. Come
             on. *(Rubbing Danielle's back)* Get it all up.
             I know you've been drinking. I know my
             vodka's been going missing. Your poor
             young body can't take it see, love.

TOMMY: *(Shouting from off stage)* Debs? Debs, you
             coming to bed, or what?

DANIELLE #2: *(Pushing Debs off and wiping her mouth on her
             sleeve)* You? Of all people? **You're** going
             to lecture me about drinking? It's not the
             drink, Mam. It's not the drink that's made
             me sick. It's you! You and your corned beef
             pie. Your joke of a fucking corned beef pie!

DANIELLE #1 enters dressed as CHAZ from Tony Hart's Take
Hart, *dragging TOMMY by his hair, and slamming his head on
the kitchen table. DANIELLE #3, dressed as MORPH from the
same production enters and punches DEBORAH in the stomach.*

13. LIVING ROOM, TERRACED HOUSE, TONYPANDY, 1993

DEBORAH: Danielle? Danielle?

TOMMY: No, it's me, Debs.

TOMMY: Bloody hell, love. How much have you had?

DEBORAH: What's it got to do with you? You're my husband not my father.

TOMMY: I'm only saying, love.

DEBORAH: Well don't say, right? It's got piss all to do with you. You don't know what it's like to be me.

TOMMY: *(Exhausted)* Are you hungry then, love? I'll get us some chips.

DEBORAH: Shove your chips up your arse, Tommy Simcox.

DANIELLE #1 crosses the stage singing 'Big Spender'.

14. BACK GARDEN, TERRACED HOUSE, TONYPANDY, 1992

DEBORAH is lying on a sun lounger, wearing a bikini and sunglasses. CRAIG and LEON are in school uniform sitting around her with glasses of lemonade in their hands, looking slightly worried.

LEON: How long do you think she'll be, Mrs Davies? See, we like to be up there early, by four or the boys from Dinas take up all the best swings.

DEBORAH: Oh, she won't be long now. Gone down the Wishing Well for new pencils or something. She's a glutton for that drawing of hers, isn't she? I used to go out with an artist once. Used to be his life model, I did. *(The boys giggle)* Hey, don't laugh, I was good at it. He did hundreds of sketches of me. Drink your lemonade now. I don't give my lemonade to anyone. I like to save it to go with my drinks. *(The boys drink their lemonade. DEBORAH adjusts her bikini.)*

CRAIG: Perhaps we should go, Mrs Davies. Tell Danielle to meet us up there. She'll know where we are.

DEBORAH: *(Sits up, pushes her sunglasses onto her head)* Oh, don't go yet. I'm enjoying your company, boys. She won't be long now. Tell you what; you couldn't give me a hand? *(Lifts a bottle of suntan lotion, passes it to LEON.)* See, I can't reach my back. *(Turns onto her stomach. The boys stare at each other)* Come on, sweetheart, or I'll be burnt to a crisp.

LEON starts working haphazardly on her shoulders.

DEBORAH: That smells nice, doesn't it? Like summer. Delicious. Coconut flavour. *(Craning her head to look at CRAIG)* Can someone do my legs too?

CRAIG: Not me, Mrs Davies. I have to go. *(Drinking his lemonade)*

LEON: Don't be chicken, Craig. *(Makes chicken noises under his breath)*

DEBORAH: I won't bite you, sweetheart. Hey, what's that? On your neck? Come here, let me have a look. *(Sits up and pats the lounger, beckoning CRAIG. CRAIG goes hesitantly. DEBORAH inspects his neck)* Blackhead. Let me get it. *(Puts her arms around him.)* This weather is brilliant for picking blackheads. See, your skin here *(massaging his neck)*, all hot and moist, it'll just slide right out in one go. Here. *(Starts squeezing. LEON is snorting with laughter)*

DANIELLE #2 enters, walking towards them but looking down at her drawing pad.

DANIELLE #2: Mam? Ma-am? They had them. A2, acid
free. *(Looks up to see the boys)*

CRAIG: *(Jumps up. Picks his skateboard up)* We came
to call for you, Dan. We're going boarding
up Clydach Hill. Hang around the park for
a bit?

DANIELLE #2: *(To her mother, screaming)* You fucking
nymphomaniac slut. You can't keep your
hands to yourself for one minute. You even
have to try it on with my school friends.
Find someone your own age. *(To CRAIG)*
Fuck off. Just fuck off. *(Runs into house)*

The boys look at DEBORAH.

DEBORAH: *(Shrugging nonchalant. To CRAIG)* Must be
her time of the month or something, kiddo.

_____

*CHAZ enters dragging TOMMY by the hair, slams his head
against the microwave table. MORPH enters and punches
DEBORAH in the stomach. WONDER WOMAN enters,
strangles DEBORAH with the cord of the iron and leaves. Slams
iron down.*

15. LIVING ROOM, TERRACED HOUSE, TONYPANDY, 1992

DEBORAH and TOMMY sit at opposite sides of the settee.
DEBORAH's drinking vodka, TOMMY's drinking beer. They're
listening to loud music. ['In the Air Tonight' by Phil Collins]

TOMMY: *(Shouting over the music)* Know what this
                  song's about? *(Pause. DEBORAH doesn't*
                  answer) It's a true story, see, about when
                  Phil Collins was at this party at this record
                  executives house in LA and everyone
                  there's plastered out of their skulls on coke,
                  like. Early in the morning when everyone's
                  pretty much comatose, he looks out the
                  window and sees one of these record
                  exec's holding this other guy down in the
                  pool. One of them liver-shaped pools, like.
                  Anyway the guy drowned, right, but the
                  record exec made out like it was because
                  the guy was out of it on drugs. Phil Collins
                  never said anything. Probably didn't want
                  to mess his contract up or whatever. Then,
                  years later, Phil Collins sees this record exec
                  in the crowd at one of his shows. And he
                  starts singing the song to him. Straight into
                  his eyes, like. Spotlight on him, everything.
                  (Singing:) **Well if you told me you were**
                  drowning, I would not lend a hand. I've

seen your face before my friend, but I don't know if you know who I am. Well I was there and I saw what you did, I saw it with my own two eyes. So you can wipe off that grin, I know where you've been. It's all been a pack of lies. *(Air drumming to the drum solo)*

DEBORAH ignores him, unimpressed, and finishes her glass of vodka. She pours herself another.

TOMMY: Love? What's wrong? Why don't you talk to me about your sister's? What's the big secret? Problem shared problem halved. All that.

DEBORAH: Huh. What's there to say? Eating biscuits in Bridgend, she is. Tapped, see. Started off she had a thing about germs. She'd let the next door neighbour in to use her phone but then afterwards she wouldn't touch it in case she caught some disease. She had to wait for her fella to come home to clean it. She'd leave it ringing all day, just ringing and ringing. Then she tried to strangle herself with the cord because she couldn't stand the ringing. Stupid cow. *(TOMMY's lost interest and is nodding again to the music. DEBORAH notices this but continues)* That's what happens when you open up. Couldn't keep it zipped, poor cow. Same with my other sister. Living on some estate in England somewhere, Lesbos manhater. *(Laughs bitterly)* You open Pandora's box and it all starts coming out. Then you can't get it all back in again. *(Shouts)* Tom! Put your bloody headphones on. This noise is getting on my tits! Worse than Danielle with your music, you are! Worse than a fifteen-year-old.

TOMMY: *(Too loudly)* You don't know what you're missing, love. Better than Bassey any day.

DEBORAH: I was my father's favourite. Course I was. Wasn't my sister was it? Poor cow. Big fat legs and massive tits. Looked unnatural on a twelve-year-old. And not my little sister. Like a little boy she was. She had a thing about these shirts. Men's shirts with big pointy collars. The Lesbos in her probably. I was the pretty one, wasn't I? Turned heads, I did. I was my father's favourite. 'Til I married Jerry Davies. Lot of good that did me. He wanted me cooped up in the house all day, cooking. Party girl, I am. He kept accusing me of sleeping with the bank manager. Got bored of taking the rap for something I didn't do. So I had an affair with the electric meter bloke. Serves his right for banging on about Elizabeth bastard Taylor day in, day out. *(Shouts)* Fat Jewish tart.

TOMMY: Love? You sure you're alright?

DEBORAH: I'm al-fucking-right, mun. Stop asking me that.

TOMMY: Well, the risotto thing. That was a bit harsh, wasn't it? You know what she said, about you being jealou—

DEBORAH: Don't you fucking start now, Tommy. *(Beat.)* Jealous? Course I'm fuckin' jealous. Skin like a peach. Waist like a bloody washboard. She doesn't even know the power she's got. I know. Eighteen inch waist I had on

50

my wedding day. They don't look at me
anymore. They look at her. She doesn't even
notice. She doesn't even know it yet.

TOMMY: *(Pulls his headphones off excitedly, points
              at the noise coming from them)* Pink Floyd.
              'Shine On You Crazy Diamond'. Bloody
              amazing, this track. I met Syd Barrett once,
              see. Fucking nutter. It was in this little bar
              in Cambridge. *(Beat.)* He was drinking a
              pint of his own piss.

DEBORAH: Never.

TOMMY: Aye. His own bloody piss, mind. With a
              Rémy Martin chaser. Whatever the hell that
              is.

16. KITCHEN, TERRACED HOUSE, TONYPANDY, 1987

DANIELLE #2: What're you doing?

DANIELLE #1: *(Defensive)* Drawing.

DANIELLE #2: You're drawing her?

DANIELLE #1: She's beautiful.

DANIELLE #2: You think?

DANIELLE #1: Yeah. She looks like a princess. Look at her.

DANIELLE #2: Why don't you draw me instead? I'll be your life model. *(Smiles, strikes a pose.)*

DANIELLE #1: You're not the same.

DANIELLE #2: What? I'm not beautiful?

DANIELLE #1: Not like her.

DANIELLE #2: But I'm here though. Where's she? In the pub. She's always in the pub. You need that picture to remind yourself what she looks like. I'm always here though, just a step ahead of you. You going to draw a picture of me or what?

DANIELLE #1: It's not the same! She's got nice hair, and green eyes, and pretty shoes. You're — *(gestures at DANIELLE #2's motorbike boots)* different.

DANIELLE #2: You know that being pretty isn't all it's cracked up to be, right? You don't have to be pretty to draw a good picture, do you?

DANIELLE #1: No, but you need to be pretty to get a husband.

DANIELLE #2: Who wants a husband?

DANIELLE #1: Everyone has to have a husband.

DANIELLE #2: Who told you that? You don't have to have a husband. Some women don't have husbands. Catwoman hasn't got a husband.

DANIELLE #1: She goes out with Batman.

DANIELLE #2: Batman hates Catwoman.

DANIELLE #1: He loves her sometimes.

DANIELLE #2: OK, bad example. Wonder Woman, then. Wonder Woman hasn't got a husband. She doesn't want a husband. What does Wonder Woman want with a husband? All he'd do is try to put his arm around her all the time, snap her bra strap, ask her what colour her knickers are.

DANIELLE #1: Is she a lesbos?

DANIELLE #2: No! And anyway, it doesn't matter. What I'm trying to tell you is that it isn't important to be pretty. There's other things you can be.

DANIELLE #1: Ugly.

DANIELLE #2: No. Nobody's ugly. You can be clever. You can have a nice personality and make people feel happy. See, if you listen to Mammy she'll tell you that all you need is good looks. A bit of charm. But that's not true, is it? She reckons she's prettier than Liz Taylor, that her fandooly drips pure liquid honey, but all she's got is Tommy Simcox, a liar with one arm longer than the other. Because she's not pretty on the inside. You only get pretty on the inside by not worrying too much about the outside. Get it? *(Stands up)* Come on, I want to show you something. *(Plugs an iron in)*.

DANIELLE #1: What are you doing?

DANIELLE #2: I'm going to show you how to iron your school uniform.

DANIELLE #1: Why?

DANIELLE #2: Because you're getting to that age when you'll start to look around at your school friend's clothes and wonder why they're neat and tidy and yours aren't. *(Ironing a shirt together)* See, when I was your age I couldn't work out why all the girls had V-neck imprints on the backs of their jumpers. Turned out their mother's ironed their clothes. There you are. Cuffs and collars first. Then we do the sleeves and we're halfway there. Your turn.

17. LIVING ROOM, TERRACED HOUSE, TONYPANDY, 1994.

TOMMY: You alright, love?

(DEBORAH grunts.)

TOMMY: Oh, come on love. This isn't any good, is it? Sat in all day drinking on your own? If you're missing Danielle why don't you give her a ring? You know where she is.

DEBORAH: Does it look like I'm missing that little cow?

TOMMY: Well —

DEBORAH: Having the time of my life, I am. No-one to have to wait on hand and foot. Look at me! I'm on cloud nine, mun. *(Sings)* **I, I, sing with me, 1, 2, 3, I….**

TOMMY: **I, I Who Have Nothing, I, I Who Have No One.**

TOMMY and DEBORAH sing 'I Who Have Nothing'. CRAIG helps DANIELLE #3 take her jeans off.

18. TEENAGER'S BEDROOM, TERRACED HOUSE, TONYPANDY, 1992

A suitcase is open on DANIELLE #2's bed, half filled with clothes. DEBORAH and DANIELLE #2 are running around the bed, screaming at one another. As DEBORAH tries to empty the suitcase, DANIELLE #2 keeps trying to refill it.

DEBORAH: *(Screaming)* You've got no idea the heartache that man caused me. You wouldn't believe it. Burned me with cigarettes, he did. He broke my dog's leg because he was so jealous of it. That man is evil, Danielle. He is evil. *(Rolling her sleeves up to show DANIELLE the cigarette burns)*

DANIELLE #2: *(Screaming)* You're lying, Mam. There's nothing there. *(Looking at DEBORAH's arms and pushing her away.)* There's nothing there. You've told the lies so many times you've started to believe them yourself. Stop lying. It's degrading. I'm going to live with him. You can't stop me.

DEBORAH: *(Screaming)* Don't you understand? You don't understand, Danielle. I've been trying to protect you. All these years I've been trying to protect you. From him. He never cared about you, Danielle. It's only me he wanted. I'm all he cared about. Trying to protect you and this is the thanks I get.

DANIELLE #2: *(Screaming)* I don't want protecting. Fifteen, I am. I can make my own mind up. I've been looking after myself since he went anyway. Where've you been? Hiding in a bottle of vodka. Don't try to put one of your guilt trips on me. It won't work. Can't you see? I'm all grown up. I can see right through you, mother. You're pathetic. I wish you were dead.

DEBORAH: *(Screaming)* You can't see anything. You're too much like him. Too bloody soft. If you leave now I won't have you back. And you'll be sorry, Danielle. You mark my words, you'll be sorry.

DANIELLE #2: *(Screaming)* I'm not coming back. And don't come looking for me when you're old and lonely because I don't care what happens to you. You'll die lonely and alone and I won't care. I'll dance on your grave, I will. It's not like you ever loved me. You're a shit mother, you are. I should get you one of those mugs for Mother's Day. **Shittest Mother in the World. Ever.**

DANIELLE #3: That was it.

DEBORAH: How could I love you?

DANIELLE #3: That's when her head went.

DEBORAH: How could I love someone like you, so cruel and hell bent on putting me in an early grave?

DANIELLE #3: That was the ultimate betrayal, leaving her for your father.

DEBORAH: Evil, you are. Like him.

DANIELLE #3: She thought she was special.

DEBORAH: I should have listened to that bastard doctor. I should have listened to him.

DANIELLE #3: She thought her piss was wine. *(Encouraging DANIELLE #2 stage side.)* Come on, let's go.

DANIELLE #2: I don't know.

DEBORAH: Don't go, Danielle.

DANIELLE #3: Your father going was one thing. But then you.

DEBORAH: Please. Don't go

DANIELLE #3: Come on, let's go. Move. You can't go backwards. Leave her. You can't go backwards. That's not the way it works. *(Pulling her)*

19. EAST GLAMORGAN HOSPITAL, WARD 5, 1996

DEBORAH is lying in the hospital bed when DANIELLE #3 arrives.

DEBORAH: Fucking grapes. I don't like grapes. It's their skin, mun. It irritates my throat. How many times have I got to tell him? Useless sod.

(DANIELLE #3 approaches, wearing a skirt.)

DEBORAH: Better.

(DANIELLE #3 sits down.)

DEBORAH: Too short though.

DANIELLE #3: I'm a tattooist now. I've got a studio in the precinct in Ponty. It's doing well, Mam.

DEBORAH: *(Stern)* I know what you are, gul. I've heard people talking about you in the market, haven't I? Complaining about your monstrous tattoos and how ugly they look on everyone. Snakes and bloody skulls. Why couldn't you have a normal job? You know, work in a shop or something? On women as well. You've got to have a screw loose to want to mark your body like that, mun. If God wanted people to have tattoos they would have been born with them, that's what my father always said.

DANIELLE #3: That's the whole point. You can't choose what you're born with, can you? You've got your ears pierced, haven't you?

DEBORAH: It's hardly the same thing. Earrings make you pretty.

DANIELLE #3: Earrings don't make you pretty. Just like tattoos don't make you ugly. It's about identity, individuality. This woman I had in today had been married for fifteen years to a loser from up Glinc, violent, unfaithful. She got her divorce papers through yesterday. She wanted the matter number tattooed under her shoulder blade. Then in block capitals underneath, *(shapes her hands around the words)* 'no more lies.'

DEBORAH: No shame, gul. Washing their dirty linen in public. What'll people think when they see her in her cossie on Porthcawl beach? 'Lesbos' they'll think. Butch old lesbos.

DANIELLE #3: Some people don't care what other people think. That's the difference between you and me, Mam. If I did I'd be in trouble. Talk of the town I was. 'There goes that alkie's daughter, skinnier than a budgie's leg. She don't feed her properly, see.' Because that's what they were really saying, wasn't it? Everywhere I went I saw the pity in their eyes. You thought you were the centre of attention, that people envied you. Pity! It was pity. Where did it get you, Mam? All the vodka, all the lies? Cirrhosis of the liver, that's where. Forty-four years old and laid out on your death bed.

(Noticing DEBORAH's foot and pulling back, feeling guilty. Clicks her tongue) Look at your foot. Does it hurt?

DEBORAH: 'Course it bloody hurts. Everything hurts. That's why I'm here. Can't get a pair of shoes on now. What do I need shoes for, anyway? I'm not going anywhere. Hey, you can have my shoes when I've gone. You always wanted them when you were little.

DANIELLE #1 crosses the stage, taking her trainers off.

DANIELLE #1: Stupid bloody things!

DEBORAH: Prettier than them. You might find yourself a nice boyfriend if you wore better shoes.

DANIELLE #3: I've got a boyfriend. You were always so obsessed with your shoes.

DEBORAH: *(Accusatory)* So were you!

MR MORGAN enters, following DANIELLE #1.

DANIELLE #1: Bore da Mr Morgan.

MR MORGAN: Interesting shoes, Danielle.

DANIELLE #1: Thanks Sir.

MR MORGAN: Not for school though. Take them off.

DANIELLE #1: *(Disappointed)* Oh, sir!

MR. MORGAN:*(Mimicking her)* Oh, sir!

20. TATTOO PARLOUR, PONTYPRIDD, 1996

DANIELLE #3: *(Smiling)* There you are, then. If you can pay at the desk. Receptionist's got your details.

TOMMY: There you are, lovely.

DANIELLE #3: Where else would I be?

TOMMY: Well you haven't been to the hospital for a week.

DANIELLE #3: Oh, what's the point, Tom? She doesn't want me there. All she does is criticise me. I'm busy here. Fifteen sittings today alone. Tribal's the thing now. Thick, black. They take forever.

TOMMY: It's worse, lovely. She's in and out of consciousness now. It could be any time. Could be tomorrow. Could be tonight.

DANIELLE #3: She told me the liver can repair itself.

TOMMY: You've seen her, lovely. She's dying. The hospital have waived visiting hours. It could be anytime. I'm going home to change. She'll be alone for a couple of hours. It's your last chance, Dan.

DANIELLE #3: *(Angry)* What's the point in anything if she's dead? Everything I've ever done, I did for her. Everything. I did it to impress her, to annoy her, to shock her. This. *(Gestures at the studio around her)* So that she'd notice me. So that she'd love me. So that she'd hate me. Anything. So now what?

CRAIG: *(Concerned)* Dan? Dan? Danielle? *(Going to her)*

TOMMY: *(Timid)* Alright, butt? *(Sighs)*

21. KITCHEN, TERRACED HOUSE, PONTYPRIDD, 1996

DANIELLE #2 is at the kitchen table with her homework, drawing and singing to herself.

DANIELLE #2: How did you meet my mother, Dad?

JERRY: Well, now —

DANIELLE #2: In a pub?

JERRY: Outside a pub, actually. I was seeing this girl from the other valley, I was, and I took her out for a run in my new Sunbeam Tiger. Lovely car, that was. I don't know why we went through Pandy to be honest, but we did. Saturday afternoon. Sunny. I was driving past the Pandy Inn, and there in the corner of my eye: ta da. Your mother waiting at the bus stop. Yellow miniskirt, legs up to her flipping neck. I can remember it like it was yesterday, love. Out of this world, she was. Like a film star. She didn't look real. Well, I just lost control of my senses, didn't I? Lush, she was. Is that what you youngsters say these days? Lush?

DANIELLE #2: She **is** a lush, yeah.

JERRY: Well, I forgot about this poor girl in the car next to me. I slammed the brakes on and shouted out of the window: 'Where're you off to then, sexy? Waiting for a bus? Where're you off to?'

DEBORAH: Ponty…

JERRY: Your mother says, sneering at me. See, it must have been strange for your mother because this girl was sitting next to me, but I'd forgotten all about her. After I saw your mother I don't think I ever looked properly at another woman again. I shouts at Debs: 'No you're not! You're coming on a date with me!' This other girl starts swearing, calling me all the F's and B's, slamming the car door, running off down towards the De Winton fields. You couldn't blame her really.

DANIELLE #2: Bet my mother loved that.

JERRY: Well, yeah; it seemed to work. Your mother got in the car and I took her to the pictures in Ponty. Closed down now. I didn't see a minute of that film. I spent the whole afternoon staring at your mother sat next to me; the prettiest thing I'd ever seen in my life. Would have walked over hot coals for your mother, I would.

DANIELLE #2: I miss her a bit, Dad. I didn't think I would, like. But I miss the way she called me 'sweetheart' when she wanted something. I know she couldn't cook but I miss the way she put too much milk in the tea so it was cold by the second sip. Margaret puts the milk in last 'cause she's a bit posh, isn't she?

DANIELLE #3: Fucking Margaret.

DEBORAH: Get me my lipstick sweetheart will you?

JERRY: I tried to teach your mother to cook. She
              wasn't interested. You know when we were
              first together, staying in your grancha's
              house? She got up one morning saying she
              was going to cook breakfast. Next thing,
              this terrible burning smell's drifting up
              the stairs. She was only trying to boil eggs
              in the electric kettle. She used to try to
              impress me in those days. That changed
              after the wedding. She was a hell of a girl,
              your mother. All layers. Like an onion.

DANIELLE #2: Yeah. Onions make you cry, don't they?
              (Beat) Then there's the stuff I **don't** miss. Like
              when she had to go to the PTA meeting…

DEBORAH: Do I look like the kind of woman who goes
              to parent teacher meetings? Do I? Tommy's
              gone to see a comedian up the Legion. I
              could have gone up there myself. Could
              have done with a pissin' laugh.

MR MORGAN enters.

DEBORAH: Well ding fucking dong.

MR MORGAN: Ah, hello, Mrs Davies. Sorry about the
              delay; just nipped to the loo. *(Looking
              around.)* Busy night.

DEBORAH: Call me Debs, darling. We're all friends
              here, aren't we? We're all here for Danielle.

MR MORGAN: So, er, Danielle? I'm Danielle's main tutor;
              her form teacher.

DEBORAH: Lucky Danielle.

MR MORGAN: We're very impressed with your daughter,
                   Mrs Davies. *(Looking down at his notes)* She's
                   advanced in her reading. In fact, she's a
                   whole year advanced. She's recently started
                   on the year eight reading list.

DEBORAH: Naturally. She's got my beans, see.

MR MORGAN: Beans?

DEBORAH: My beans. My NDA.

MR MORGAN: *(Not making eye contact)* And she's obviously
                   blessed with a creative flair. I'm sure
                   you've seen her drawings pinned up in the
                   corridor. Some of them are highly original,
                   I must say.

DEBORAH: Oh, you must. Hot in here, isn't it? Phew.
                   I've got a mouth like an Arab's dap here.
                   (Goes in her bag for a bottle of vodka, swigs at it.)

MR MORGAN: Our concern is that Danielle is often
                   somewhat withdrawn, Mrs Davies. Quiet.
                   Not always keen to participate in group
                   activities, class discussions, that sort of
                   thing.

DEBORAH: Are you sure about that, sweetheart? She's
                   got a mouth on her in the house.

*MR MORGAN is embarrassed, searching frantically through his
notes.*

DEBORAH: I'm joking, darling. I'm teasing you. Loosen
                   up. *(Throws papers on the floor)* There you
                   are. What were you saying?

MR MORGAN: *(Picks his papers up)* Class discussions. We know she's bright. But she chooses not to engage —

DEBORAH: Well I always engage.

MR MORGAN: Confidence could be an issue here.

DEBORAH: Oh I don't think it will be love. *(Holding MR MORGAN's face)* Tell you what, handsome. Let's get out of this stuffy school hall, continue our little meeting somewhere more private?

MR MORGAN: We can't do this!

JERRY: Inappropriate.

MR MORGAN: No I really can't do this. Mrs Davies I'm going to have to ask you too leave. The door is that way, I'm going this way.

JERRY: Entirely inappropriate.

DEBORAH: What a boring bunch of bastards, you are. You wouldn't know what fun was if it turned up and shat in your laps. *(Notices a big rubber plant in the corner)* Now look at that. I've always wanted one of them. Must be my lucky day. *(Picks the plant up and dances with it, singing)* **The minute you walked in the joint, I could see you were a man of distinction, a real big spender. Good looking, so refined. Say, wouldn't you like to know what's going on in my mind. So let me get right to the point.** *(About to exit)* **I don't pop my cork for every man I see.** *(Exits)* **Hey Big Spender!**

JERRY: Yeah. She was a hell of a girl, your mother.

> *(Gets up with a sigh and goes off to make his cup of tea.)*

DANIELLE #2: *(Mortified)* Oh my fucking God. I wish she'd listened that doctor. I wish the ground would have swallowed me, I swear.

DANIELLE #3: Don't worry about it. Believe me, you'll be able to laugh about in a few years time. The funny thing is that after Dad went I used to dream she'd marry Mr Morgan. Someone stable. *(Beat.)* So how's things? With loverboy?

DANIELLE #2: *(Looks at her, taking an interest)* Craig?

DANIELLE #3: Of course, Craig. *(Rolls eyes)* Who else?

DANIELLE #2: *(Looks despondent)* I don't think he's into the whole motorbike-boot-alcoholic's-daughter sort of thing.

DANIELLE #3: *(Laughs)* You've got to take the lead. Your legs are fab, babe. Wear the short skirt. To the party on Friday.

DANIELLE #2: They're bandy. She told me.

DANIELLE #3: *(Laughs bitterly. Scrapes DANIELLE #2's hair out of her face. Look at her sadly)* They're perfect. Your legs are perfect. *(Beat.)* And he's crazy about you, sweetheart. Don't you see? He gets a semi on every time he looks at you.

DANIELLE #2: Just a semi?

JERRY: Come on then, Dan, you'd better clear this up. Look, you've got charcoal here on Margaret's best table cloth. I hope that washes out. I've cleared you a space in the spare room for you to do your drawing. Margaret'll have a fit if she sees you by here.

DANIELLE #2: Of course it washes out. It's just charcoal, Dad.

DANIELLE #3: It's not permanent. It's not like tattoo ink or anything.

JERRY: *(Looks strangely at DANIELLE #3, almost acknowledging her, but not quite. Looks to DANIELLE #2)* This is her best filet lace, love. Come on, I tipped curry sauce on it once; she had my nutsack in a knot for a fortnight.

22. KITCHEN, TERRACED HOUSE, TONYPANDY, 1992

DANIELLE #2 is sitting at the kitchen table surrounded by her art project. DEBORAH enters and goes to a mirror, fiddling with her hair and spraying hairspray.

DANIELLE #2: *(Coughing)* Mam? Can I have some money? I'm running out of paper. I need to finish this project for school.

DEBORAH: *(Opening a packet of stockings)* Doesn't the school supply that these days?

DANIELLE #2: I need it now. It's homework. I've got to finish it before I go back on Monday.

DEBORAH: *(Takes the card out of an empty stocking packet and holds it up)* This any good?

DANIELLE #2: Don't be stupid. It's for school. It's important.

DEBORAH: Well you never minded before.

DANIELLE #2: I did mind, actually. All I wanted was real paper, like normal kids. How much is a pad anyway? It's cheaper than a pair of stockings. But you've got to have your stockings, haven't you. All I get is this.

(Rips the card in two)

DEBORAH: You're so bloody ungrateful. Doesn't matter if I bought you all the paper in the world, you'd still be painting on everything in the house with my best nail polish. Normal kids don't go around painting on the furniture with their mother's best nail varnish, not at fifteen.

DANIELLE #2: No. 'Cause normal kids got paper. Normal kids got acrylic paints. Normal kids got normal mothers.

DEBORAH: Money doesn't grow on trees, girl.

DANIELLE #2: Money does grow on trees, Mam. It's paper, isn't it? *(Makes a face at her mother.)* I'd get a paper round but you won't let me. Reckon I'll get molested. It's not that though, is it? You just want to have total control over me. You don't want me to have any money. It's only paper I want, mun. It's not like I'm asking for money for the school skiing trip, or my first new uniform in two years, or a bottle of vodka. Two flippin' pound. For a flippin' drawing pad. So I can actually pass my exam.

DEBORAH: Oh, I declare, Danielle. I really do.

DANIELLE #2: Yeah? I declare as well. *(Putting her things away in a pencil case)* I'm going down Nanna and Grancha's. They'll buy me paper.

DEBORAH: Don't you dare go down there, begging. Don't you ever go down there. Don't you dare! *(Quieter)* Don't you ever go down there.

DANIELLE #2: Well I need it for school. I'll get in trouble otherwise.

DEBORAH: Look, I'll buy you the bloody paper. Stop
             your mingeing, alright? I'll get some money
             off Tommy later, you can get it tomorrow.

DANIELLE #2: Mingeing? What the fuck? *(Staring at DEBS)*

DEBORAH: Danielle! Stop your swearing. Give me
             some peace to get ready. You can have your
             pad tomorrow. Jesus wept.

23. LIVING ROOM, TERRACED HOUSE, TONYPANDY, 1995

DEBORAH is curled on the floor when TOMMY arrives home from work.

TOMMY: Debs? Deborah? *(Getting hold of her and trying to raise her onto the sofa)* Come on, love. Up we get.

DEBORAH: *(Shouting, barely coherent)* Danni? Danni?

TOMMY: It's me, love. Come on.

DEBORAH: *(Trying to wrestle him off but she's too weak)* Get off me. Get off me. I'm OK.

TOMMY: *(Looking around in desperation, still holding his nose)* You're not, love. You're ill. You're really ill and you've— *(pointing at her to indicate she's soiled herself)* I'm phoning the doctor. I have to.

DEBORAH: I don't need no fucking doctor. Leave me alone.

TOMMY: But you do, love. I'm sorry, love. You do. *(Going to the phone)*

24. EAST GLAMORGAN HOSPITAL, WARD 5, 1996

DEBORAH: *(Struggling to speak)* Where've you been? I haven't seen you.

DANIELLE #3: I'm sorry, Mam. I've been busy. Work things.

NURSE: Not so good today. Can I get you anything from the trolley? A coffee?

DANIELLE #3: No. Thank you. *(Beat.)* You never told me you loved me. You never told me anything. Not one positive thing my entire life. What harm would it have done to encourage me? To tell me you were proud?

DEBORAH: *(Eyes closed and struggling)* You didn't need any encouragement.

DANIELLE #3: You rejected me. That made me love you more. I loved you so much I could have choked on it. No one loved you more than me.

DEBORAH: **You** left.

DANIELLE #3: I would have strangled you.

DEBORAH: I made you strong.

DANIELLE #3: You made me hard.

DEBORAH: It's the same thing.

DANIELLE #3: No, it's not Mam. Admitting something doesn't make you weak. Telling your own child that you love them doesn't make you weak. Having feelings, being human, that doesn't make you weak. Say it. Tell me you love me.

TOMMY: Dan? You OK, lovely? I'll take over now if you want.

DANIELLE #3: Yeah. Yeah, I have to go.

DEBORAH: Danni? You smell nice, sweetheart. New perfume?

DANIELLE #3: No.

DEBORAH: Oh, it smells nice. You smell nice, sweetheart. See you tomorrow, is it?

DANIELLE #3: *(Putting on a brave face)* Yep, see you tomorrow.

Lights lowered.

DANIELLE #3: *(To Audience)* I saw her the next day. But she didn't see me. From the corner I watched her. Tommy was holding her hand. I thought she was too mean to die. And if she did die, I thought the world would end. That everything would explode.

DANIELLE #2: But there was no trouble.

DANIELLE #3: No bother.

DANIELLE #1: No Tonypandemonium.

DANIELLE #3: She slipped away, easy as a leaf falling
from a tree. I looked around and everything
was the same. *(They hold hands)*

DANIELLE #3: The dinner lady was doing her rounds,
whistling a tune.

DANIELLE #1: And when it happened the dinner lady
didn't stop whistling.

DANIELLE #2: She just kept on going, whistling.

DANIELLE #3: And the clock kept chiming, like the world
wasn't exploding, like the world would
keep on going.

ALL DANIELLE'S:
And the world just kept on going.

DANIELLE #1: Yep. We just kept on going.

'a feat of modern playwriting brilliance'
South Wales Echo

'Tragic yet touching stuff ... sensitive, stylish, emotive'
Buzz Magazine

'a deeply moving, dark emotional train wreck of a story but one also filled with humour and an ultimate message of love.'
Theatre Wales

'a heartfelt, well crafted and brave piece of work which is no doubt the start of Trezise's successful career as a playwright.'
Western Mail

PHOTOSECTION

Sarah Williams as Danielle #3 and Berwyn Pearce as Craig.

Adam Redmore as Tommy and Siwan Morris as Deborah.

Siwan Morris as Deborah.

Adam Redmore as Tommy.

Siwan Morris as Deborah, Molly Elson as Danielle #2
and Berwyn Pearce as Craig (?)

Siwan Morris as Deborah.

PARTHIAN

Drama Titles

9781905762811	9.99	*Black Beach*	Coca, Jordi; Casas, Joan; Cunillé, Lluïsa, Teare, Jeff (ed.)
9781905762859	7.99	*Blink*	Rowlands, Ian
9781902638966	7.99	*Butterfly*	Rowlands, Ian
9781902638539	6.99	*Football*	Davies, Lewis
9781905762590	9.99	*Fuse*	Jones, Patrick
9781902638775	7.99	*Hijinx Theatre*	Cullen, Greg; Morgan, Sharon; Davies, Lewis; Hill, Val (ed.)
9781906998547	8.99	*House of America*	Thomas, Ed
9780952155867	6.99	*Merthyr Trilogy, The*	Osborne, Alan
9781902638416	7.99	*More Lives than One*	Jenkins, Mark
9781902638799	7.99	*Mother Tongue*	Williams, Roger
9780952155874	6.99	*New Welsh Drama 1*	Malik, Afshan; Williams, Roger; Davies, Lewis, Teare, Jeff (ed.)
9781902638133	5.99	*New Welsh Drama 2*	Evans, Siân; Smith, Othniel; Williams, Roger; Teare, Jeff (ed.)
9781902638355	7.99	*New Welsh Drama 3*	Ross, Lesley; Davies, Lewis; Morgan, Chris (ed.)
9781902638485	9.99	*Now You're Talking*	Davies, Hazel Walford (ed.)
9781908069962	8.99	*Protagonists, The*	Chamberlain, Brenda; Davies, Damian Walford (ed.)
9781902638638	7.99	*Seeing Without Light*	Turley, Simon
9781902638249	9.99	*Selected Work '95-'98*	Thomas, Ed
9781906998363	7.99	*State of Nature*	Turley, Simon
9781902638669	7.99	*Still Life*	Way, Charles
9781906998585	9.99	*Strange Case of Dr Jekyll and Mr Hyde as Told to Carl Jung by an Inmate of Broadmoor Asylum, The*	Mark, Ryan
9781902638478	7.99	*Transitions: New Welsh Drama IV*	Morgan, Chris (ed.)
9781902638010	6.99	*Trilogy of Appropriation, A*	Rowlands, Ian